LEGENDARY GREEK NAMES

ORPHEUS
&
EURYDICE

JILL DUDLEY

PUT IT IN YOUR POCKET SERIES
ORPINGTON PUBLISHERS

Published by
Orpington Publishers

Cover design and origination by
Creeds, Bridport, Dorset
01308 423411

Printed and bound in the UK by
Creeds

© Jill Dudley 2023

ISBN: 978-0-9955781-8-0

ORPHEUS & EURYDICE

Orpheus was believed to have been the son either of Apollo, or the Thracian river-god Oigros. His mother was the Muse Calliope, Muse of epic poetry. Calliope's parents were Zeus, supreme god of the ancient world, and Mnemosyne whose name means 'memory' – a vital faculty in the human make-up. Together Zeus and Mnemosyne had nine offspring, each one a Muse and goddess of one of the fine arts.

Orpheus grew up in Thrace, in the north-east of Greece which borders with Turkey, and became renowned for his singing and his playing of the lyre. In fact his voice was said to be so beautiful that the mountains and trees bowed down to him, animals drew near, and fish rose up from the sea to listen.

As a young man Orpheus joined Jason* and the Argonauts on their quest to recover the Golden Fleece. It was Cheiron, the wise and gentle Centaur (half-man, half-horse) who lived in a cave on Mt. Pelion, who recommended that the Argonauts take Orpheus along with them because of his fine voice.

And Cheiron was right. It turned out that during the voyage Orpheus' singing proved to be invaluable as it soothed frayed tempers, calmed the waves, and outshone the Siren

Voices (women who lured mariners to their certain deaths by the beauty of their song). Some say it was Orpheus, and not Medea with her sorcery and witchcraft, who helped Jason steal the Golden Fleece from the holy grove of Ares, god of war, because with his voice Orpheus was able to lull to sleep the ever wakeful dragon/serpent who guarded it.

On his return to Greece Orpheus fell in love and married Eurydice, a lovely Dryad (a tree-nymph). Orpheus was passionately in love with his new bride, but tragedy struck when Eurydice, fleeing across a meadow from Aristaeus (a son of Apollo with amorous intentions) was bitten by a snake and died.

Orpheus was overwhelmed with grief at never seeing his beloved Eurydice again. In his despair he made his way down to the underworld in search of his dead bride. Faced with Charon (the ferry-man who ferried the dead across the river Styx), and Cerberus (the three-headed guard-dog who savaged any would-be escapee from Hades), Orpheus began to sing and play his lyre; he did it so beautifully that he charmed Charon and Cerberus who fawned with pleasure and allowed Orpheus to pass down to the dreaded subterranean kingdom of the dead.

When Hades (and his queen, Persephone), heard Orpheus approaching, they too were won over by his song. Feeling sorry for the young devoted husband they granted him his wish and allowed Eurydice back to the upper world. They said she could return with him but only on the one condition that he led the way and never looked back to see if she was following.

Overjoyed, Orpheus took his bride by the hand.

Unfortunately, in his great joy and excitement, as he approached the upper world again, he glanced back to reassure himself she was still there. It was a fatal error because Eurydice immediately faded and became condemned for ever as a shade in the underworld.

Orpheus was inconsolable by his loss, and from then on shunned all women preferring only the company of men. He had always been a devotee of the god Dionysos, god of wine and drama, who was much worshipped in the area and the foothills of Mt. Olympus. The god's followers were mainly women known as Maenads whose worship of Dionysos caused them to fall into ecstatic frenzies. During such ecstasies their custom was to run up into the mountains dressed in fawnskins, each carrying a flaming torch and a thyrsos (a staff wrapped around with ivy or vine tendrils, topped by a pine-cone). In their frenetic state they were able to tear apart wild beasts and devour them.

When Orpheus set himself apart and would have nothing more to do with these Maenads, they turned on him and, in their wild frenzy tore him limb from limb leaving them with blood-stained hands which they washed in the pure water of a Mt. Olympus river. Horrified by such sacrilege the river vanished underground, and did not resurface till it reached the sacred site of Dion some four miles away. Others say that the remains of Orpheus were buried by his family in the foothills of Mt. Olympus near a town named Leibethra. Later an oracle pronounced that if ever his bones saw the sun then the town would be destroyed. Not long afterwards, there was an earthquake and his tomb was overturned and the sun shone down on his bones. The town of Leibethra was washed away, so fulfilling the oracle's prophecy.

Other reports claim that the inhabitants of Dion gathered up the bones of Orpheus and re-buried them, and his tomb was still standing at the time of Pausanias, the second century A.D. historian, who reported: *If you leave Dion by the road towards the mountain, when you have gone twenty stades you see on your right a column with an urn set upon it. According to the local story, the urn contains the bones of Orpheus.*

Another story, however, states that the head of Orpheus was thrown into a river on Mt. Olympus, and his head (still singing, together with his lyre), floated downstream to the Aegean sea. There it was carried on the tide till it was washed up on the island of Lesbos in the Aegean sea. It is no surprise that the island later became renowned for its music and its poetry, Sappho being a name that is remembered to this day.

Continuing with the Maenad legend, the head of Orpheus, on arriving at ancient Antissa on Lesbos, floated upriver till it reached a cave. There it installed itself and became known for its oracular pronouncements. Many people came to consult it, and its fame quickly spread. One day, however, Apollo heard of this new oracle site, and was greatly angered that his own oracular powers at Delphi were in danger of being superceded. He put an immediate stop to such impertinence, one report asserting that Apollo stood over the head of Orpheus, and said: 'Cease from the things that are mine, for I have borne enough with thy singing'.

From Orpheus came the ancient Greek mystic religion known as Orphism, thought to have originated in the seventh or sixth century B.C. It was based on poems attributed to Orpheus advocating the repeated purification of the individual soul till it eventually attained perfection and broke free from its 'grievous circle' of reincarnations.

Orpheus was the very antithesis of the heroes or warriors of antiquity. Rather he was a man of peace, of music and poetry and gentleness.

It is interesting that Christ, the Son of God, preached love and peace but died a violent death as Orpheus did. And astonishing that there exists today an early image of a crucified body nailed to a cross which one would suppose was an image of the crucified Christ, except that below the cross is inscribed in Greek the words 'Orpheus – Bakkikoc' – 'Bakkikoc' being a variant of Bacchus, another name for Dionysos.

The use of mythological figures in art was often deliberately adopted by the Christians to ease the pagan mind into the new Christian religion. Alternatively, it may have been a Christian way suggesting death to Orphism, except that many scholars think the visual crucifixion predates Christianity.

A happier imitation of Christ taken from a pagan statue of Orpheus is one of Orpheus with a sheep slung across his shoulders. In the Christian era it represents Christ the good shepherd and illustrates the parable of the lost sheep.

Today, when the name of Orpheus is mentioned, it is linked with Eurydice. The tragic loss of his wife and his effort to bring her back to life has ever since been a popular subject for poets and for tragic opera. Thanks to Mnemosyne, Orpheus' maternal grandmother, the memory of Orpheus remains eternal.

Denotes a separate booklet on the subject.

GLOSSARY

APOLLO – Son of Zeus and Leto, and twin brother of Artemis, goddess of the hunt. He was god of music, archery and prophecy.

ARISTAEUS – A son of Apollo. He was the cause of Eurydice's death because she trod on a venomous snake in fleeing from him when he was pursuing her.

BACCHUS – see Dionysos.

BACCHAE – see Maenads.

CALLIOPE – One of the nine Muses, and mother of Orpheus. His father is generally thought to be Apollo. She was the Muse of epic poetry.

CERBERUS – The monster dog standing guard at the entrance to Hades. He had three heads, a snake's tail and snake heads along his back.

CHARON – The ferryman who ferried the dead across the river Styx to Hades.

CHEIRON – A centaur, half-man, half-horse. Unlike other centaurs who were unruly, lascivious creatures, Cheiron was wise and kind, and knowledgeable in medicine, the arts and music.

DIONYSOS – Son of Zeus and the mortal beauty Semele. He was god of wine and drama. The Romans called him Bacchus.

EURYDICE – A Dryad (tree-nymph) whom Orpheus fell passionately in love with and married. Tragically, soon after her marriage, she was pursued by Aristaeus and, while escaping from his clutches, she trod on a venomous snake and died.

HADES – Brother of Zeus and god of the underworld. His queen was Persephone, daughter of Demeter, goddess of corn and agriculture.

HOMER – Greek epic poet who composed the *Iliad* and the *Odyssey*. He was believed to have lived c.700 B.C.

JASON – Son of Aeson, the rightful king of Iolchos, whose throne was usurped by Pelias. The latter promised to give up the throne if Jason brought him back the Golden Fleece from Colchis

MAENADS – Women followers of Dionysos who, under his divine power, were seized with superhuman strength and, in a state of ecstatic frenzy, ran into the mountains where they tore apart wild beasts and devoured them.

MEDEA – Daughter of King Aeetes of Colchis. Thanks to her witchcraft and sorcery, she helped Jason retrieve the Golden Fleece.

MNEMOSYNE – A personification of Memory, and mother of the Muses by Zeus.

MUSES – The nine daughters of Zeus and Mnemosyne. Each presided over one of the arts or sciences.

PAUSANIAS – A Greek traveller and writer of the second century A.D. and author of *Guide to Greece*, Volumes 1 (Central Greece) and Volume 2 (Southern Greece).

PERSEPHONE – Daughter of Zeus and Demeter. She was abducted by Hades and became his queen in the underworld where she remained for four months of the year, returning to Demeter for the other eight months.

ZEUS – Supreme god of the ancient world. He was married to Hera, but had numerous extra-marital affairs with mortal and immortal beauties, by whom he fathered many gods and demi-gods.

MORE FROM THE PUT IT IN YOUR POCKET SERIES:

GREEK MYTHS
THE JUDGEMENT OF PARIS
HELEN
KING AGAMEMNON
ACHILLES
THE WOODEN HORSE
ODYSSEUS

ISLANDS
CHIOS – HOMER
CRETE – THESEUS AND THE MINOTAUR
DELOS – BIRTHPLACE OF APOLLO
ITHAKA – ODYSSEUS
KOS – HIPPOCRATES AND ASCLEPIUS
LESBOS (MYTILENE) – SAPPHO AND ORPHEUS
NAXOS – THESEUS AND THE MINOTAUR
PATMOS – ST. JOHN THE THEOLOGIAN
RHODES – THE COLOSSUS
SAMOS – PYTHAGORAS AND THE HERAION
SANTORINI – THE LOST ISLAND OF ATLANTIS
TINOS – THE MIRACLE-WORKING ICON

SACRED SITES
ATHENS – THE ACROPOLIS
ELEUSIS – DEMETER AND KORE
EPIDAURUS – CENTRE OF HEALING
DELPHI – THE ORACLE OF APOLLO
CORINTH – ST. PAUL AND THE GODDESS OF LOVE
OLYMPIA – THE OLYMPIC GAMES

ALSO BY JILL DUDLEY:

YE GODS!
(TRAVELS IN GREECE)

YE GODS! II
(MORE TRAVELS IN GREECE)

HOLY SMOKE!
(TRAVELS IN TURKEY AND EGYPT)

GODS IN BRITAIN
(AN ISLAND ODYSSEY FROM PAGAN TO CHRISTIAN)

MORTALS AND IMMORTALS
(A SATIRICAL FANTASY & TRUE-IN-PARTS MEMOIR)

HOLY FIRE!
(TRAVELS IN THE HOLY LAND)

LAP OF THE GODS
(TRAVELS IN CRETE AND THE AEGEAN ISLANDS)

GODS & HEROES
(ON THE TRAIL OF THE ILIAD & THE ODYSSEY)

BEHIND THE MASKS
(IN THE FOOTSTEPS OF THE EARLY GREEK DRAMATISTS)

OH, SOCRATES!
(TRACKING THE LIFE AND DEATH OF SOCRATES)